Dedicated to my wonderful husband, Marcus, who has encouraged me to hold fast to the truth of God's word through times when I didn't think I could hold on much longer.

Introduction

The dream of writing a book was put into my heart 10 years ago. I wasn't sure what that book would be about – I actually thought it would be more of a children's book – or a youth historical novel based on the book Esther. That might still happen one day since the dream for it is still present. But God put another vision for a book that felt more achievable for a first publication – a 30-day devotional. As I was reading God's word, I noticed an interesting theme – holding fast, or standing fast. I was intrigued by this theme and as I continued to read, I would come across it again and again. I felt the prompting of the Holy Spirit telling me this was the topic for my devotional.

In a world that tugs and pulls at us for our attention, we need to remember to whom we are to hold on to, to whom we must rest in and from whom our strength is found in. My hope and prayer is that this devotional will serve that purpose – a reminder for us.

I also wanted this devotional to consist of short readings that get to the heart. In some days, I talk about marriage. If you are a single woman (or a man), feel free to mentally change it to where you feel God is directing you. I also wrote this devotional with women in mind. If you are a man reading this devotional, please keep that in mind…and let me know what you think!

Day One

Colossians 1:21-23

"And you, who once were alienated and enemies in your mind by wicked works, yet now He has reconciled in the body of His flesh through death, to present you holy, and blameless, and above reproach in His sight if indeed you continue in the faith, grounded and *steadfast*, and are not moved away from the hope of the gospel which you heard, which was preached to every creature under heaven, of which, I, Paul, became a minister."

It can be so easy to get distracted by earthly desires. Gurus of all kinds hand out promises to the hurting like lollipops. We will grasp at anything that will give us any kind of hope, even when we know it is just temporary hope. When that fleeting hope fades, we'll be on the lookout for a new hope. And the brutal cycle continues. It is only when we trust in the true hope of Jesus Christ that we acquire our eternal and everlasting hope. In this passage, Paul is urging us to be steadfast in the hope that the gospel brings - the only true and endless hope. Through the sacrifice that Christ made, through giving up His body, we have been reconciled to God. Remaining steadfast in this hope will allow us the opportunity to be presented to God holy and blameless; beyond reproach. Now that is hope! Let us not be moved away from the hope Jesus has freely given.

Prayer

Heavenly Father.

Thank you for the ultimate hope we have in Your Son, Jesus Christ. Thank you that through Jesus, we can come before You, holy and blameless. Our sins have been washed white as snow. Please help me to not move away from this perfect hope.

In Your name, Jesus,

Amen

Day Two

Philippians 4:1

"Therefore, my beloved and longed-for brethren, my joy and crown, so stand fast in The Lord, beloved."

Right after that encouragement, Paul addresses a couple of women in the Philippian church who are having a disagreement. He urges them to be of the same mind. How often have we, as relational women, had disagreements with a sister in Christ? Clearly, the women here are creating so much tension within the church that Paul has to address them personally. He also urges other church members to get in the midst of the issue and help the women diffuse the issue. As women, we need to be so careful to not get into the middle of a disagreement and take sides. We need to be careful to not cause more dissension by meddling. In order for us to get into the midst of disunity, we must be standing fast in The Lord. We must point others to Christ and to encourage them to stand fast in The Lord as well.

Prayer

Heavenly Father,

Thank you for Your Church, for Your people. Please help us to be in unity with one another through Your Holy Spirit.

If I am in any disagreement with a sister or brother in Christ, please help me to do my part to diffuse the situation. Help me to see it through Your eyes. Give me a heart of compassion towards my sister or brother.

If there is turmoil within my church family, help me to reflect Your glory and truth to those involved. If I have engaged in the situation in an unholy way, please forgive me. Help me to always point others to You in all I do.

In Your Holy name,

Amen

Day Three

Philippians 2:14-16

"Do all things without complaining and disputing, that you may become blameless and harmless, children of God without fault in the midst of a crooked and perverse generation, among whom you shine as lights in the world, holding fast the word of life, so that I may rejoice in the day of Christ that I have not run in vain or laboured in vain."

Do ALL things without complaining!?!? Oh, dear... We live in a world that loves to complain, don't we? When was the last time you complained about something? Last week? Yesterday? This morning? Just a minute ago? Many times, we complain and we don't even realize that we are complaining. It is so ingrained in us! We complain about our homes, our cars, the bills, the cost of groceries, cost of gas, our kids complaining... We must become very aware of how often we complain about ridiculous things and STOP! Paul says that if we do all things without complaining and disputing, then we will shine as lights in the world! And, let's be honest, this world needs the Light! To stop our complaining, we need to hold fast to the word of life. What is the word of life? John 1 reveals that Jesus is the Word. He is also Life. So, we must cling to Jesus! When we feel the urge to complain, hold fast to Jesus!

Prayer

Heavenly Father,

Thank you for sending your Son so I may have Life. Thank you that He is the Word in flesh. Thank you for making a way for me to stop complaining! Please remind me of this truth when I begin to complain about the gifts you have given to me or about challenges I face. Help me to turn to You for help instead of complaining. Help me to hold fast to Your Son everyday so I will not be tempted to complain.

In Your name,

Amen

Day Four

Philippians 1:27

"Only let your conduct be worthy of the gospel of Christ, so that whether I come and see you or am absent, I may hear of your affairs, that you stand fast in one spirit , with one mind striving together for the faith of the gospel."

Although Paul, was speaking to the church in Philippi, I think this passage can be reflected upon in the area of marriage. We can certainly be in disunity with our husbands, can't we? It is so important for married couples to stand together in one spirit and one mind. This is the essence of 'leaving parents and cleaving to your spouse'. When I am not in unit with my husband, I know I need to spend time in prayer. This is easier said than done. Sometimes I just want to stay in disunity so that I can have my own way. Sometimes I am just mad. But, is this kind of behaviour worthy of the gospel of Christ? No, it clearly isn't. What have you been in disunity with your husband about? Are you quick to turn to God in prayer with these problems? Or do you hang on to them? I am working on swiftly turning to God with my issues. Can we encourage each other to do this?

Prayer

Heavenly Father,

Please forgive me for the times I have been in disunity with my husband. I know situations and decisions don't always turn out the way that I want them to. Please help me to be patient and understanding of my husband's decisions for our family. Please give my husband abundant wisdom and help me to encourage him in turning to You. Help me to let him know that I trust him with our family.

Please bless our marriage as we work at unity and one mind, as we cleave to each other. Please send Your Holy Spirit into my marriage so that we will become more as one with each other and with You.

In Your precious name, Jesus,

Amen

Day Five

Ephesians 6:14-18

"Stand therefore, having girded your waist." (You can read all of the armour of God at this time!)

Can you imagine a police officer sitting in his car, yelling at a perpetrator to stop? A trained police officer would not just sit there! He would be standing, ready to engage. How about a soldier on the front lines? Would he be sitting around, casually waiting for an enemy? NO! He would be on full alert, ready to fire! So, why should our demeanour be any different? We are in a battle! We often get so caught up in life, which we forget a spiritual battle rages on. Put on your armour every single day! Keep your armour in good condition – the enemy will find a weak spot if there is one! Be in His word, walk in the Spirit, pray often, be confident in your salvation – and in who your salvation is, invest in godly relationships, seek godly counsel, exercise your faith, be a peacemaker, use scripture in prayer, turn from sin.

Get know your armour – know the purpose for each piece – and don't be afraid to wield that sword! I have also found that many times, I need my armour to defend a fellow soldier in the army of God. And many times, my comrades have had to brandish their sword on my behalf and put their shield around me. On a very special note, the armour we have been given is the very same armour Jesus wears!! Check out Isaiah 59:17!

Prayer

Heavenly Father,

Please forgive me for the times I have not put on my armour, for not wielding the sword of the Spirit and not having faith. Please help me to keep my armour in good spiritual shape, ready to fight at any moment. Thank you so much for the gift of Your heavenly armour so that we can be protected from the enemy who wants nothing more than to destroy and kill. Please help me to build my faith in You. Show me ways in which I can use my sword for helping my friends and teach me to hold my shield over them when necessary. Put good friends in my life that will do the same for me.

In Your name, Jesus,

Amen

Day Six

Colossians 2:18-19

"Let no one cheat you of your reward, taking delight in *false* humility and worship of angels, intruding into those things which he has not seen, vainly puffed up by his fleshly mind, and not holding fast to the Head, from whom all the body, nourished and knit together by joints and ligaments, grows with the increase *that is* from God."

I am wondering if false humility and vain 'puffiness' are consequences of not holding fast to God. And I wonder if we are more easily cheated of our reward when we are not holding fast to our Heavenly Father. Perhaps this might be an outcome of pride – vanity, being puffed up. And of course, we get full of pride when we focus on ourselves and our own counterfeit righteousness. Let's continuously hold on to our Father so that we keep our pride in check!

In the previous 2 verses, Paul tells us to not worry about other people judging us in food, in drink, regarding a festival, new moon or Sabbath. We can't obtain righteousness with our diet – Jesus is our righteousness. A festival can't make you more righteous either. The Sabbath was meant to help us rest – foreshadowing Jesus and our blessing of resting in Him – so it doesn't matter which day we attend church as long as we are resting in Him. Let's embrace the reward we have in Him and not allow others to rob us of that gift. Let's hold on to the righteousness and rest we have in Christ Jesus.

When we hold fast to God, the body of Christ is nourished and knit together. What a wonderful image! Being knit together with other followers of Christ! Let's help each other hold fast to Jesus!

Prayer

Heavenly Father,

Please forgive me for the times I have been prideful in my own self-righteousness. Please give me daily reminders that my righteousness comes from Christ alone. Please forgive me for allowing others to steal the reward I have in You. Please help me to rest in You. Thank You that You are my Sabbath and I don't have to hold on to special diets and rituals for my righteousness and rest. You have freely offered all of that and more, Jesus. Please knit me together with other followers so that I can do my part in encouraging and building up the body of Christ.

In Your name Jesus,

Amen

Day Seven

1 Thessalonians 3:8

"For now we live, if you stand fast in the Lord."

Paul is speaking to the church he founded in Thessalonica. The church is struggling and yet they remain faithful. Paul is encouraged by this. Paul had sent Timothy to Thessalonica to check on the church and good news was reported back to Paul – good news of faith and love. I wonder if this encouragement helped Paul to continue on in His ministry despite hardships, persecution and imprisonment. The church's faith brought Paul encouragement through his affliction. Paul says he lives because of their steadfastness. Sometimes when we are discouraged and want to give up, our hearts begin to die. I think hearing of this church's faith and love for each other brought vivacity to Paul's heart – it got him excited. What mattered to Paul was the faith and love being exhibited by the people – not riches, not material things – but how they held on to faith and love.

Do you know someone who needs some encouragement today? If not, ask God to bring someone to mind who needs godly encouragement. How can your faith and love encourage someone in their distress? Recently, at our church family camp, an older lady came up to me and thanked me again for a note of encouragement I had sent to her several months before. She said she reads it often and feels encouraged. When God placed it upon my heart to write a note to her, I had no idea what it would mean to her. I doubted that God was wanting me to write a note to a woman I had never met. Would she even know who I was? And yet the godly encouragement I gave to her still speaks truth into her precious heart now. Amazing. Who does God want you to speak truth to today? Who can you encourage through your steadfastness in the Lord? The life God has given to you speaks volumes to those who are dying inside.

Prayer

Heavenly Father,

Thank You that You have given us the gift of abundant life through Your Son, Jesus Christ. I know there are people I know who are struggling today. Please bring people to my mind so that I may lift them up in prayer to You and perhaps send them a note of encouragement. Give me the words to say that will help start to bring life back into their hearts by the power of the Holy Spirit. Let me be an instrument of encouragement and life for You, Lord.

In Your name, Jesus,

Amen

Day Eight

2 Thessalonians 2:15

"Therefore, brethren, stand fast and hold the traditions which you were taught, whether by word or our epistle."

Paul is encouraging the Thessalonians to hang on to the teachings he has taught them. He wants them to remember the traditions he has taught them, not religious traditions that turn faith into religion and legalism. Paul is aware that there are struggles and persecution. He wants the Thessalonians to stand fast onto the word of God. In order for us to persevere and grow spiritually, we must stand firm on the word of God and the teachings within. We must have a teachable spirit – taught by both the Holy Spirit and other disciples of Christ.

Paul then goes on to say "Now may our Lord Jesus Christ Himself, and our God and Father, who has loved us and given *us* everlasting consolation and good hope by grace, comfort your hearts and establish you in every good word and work." What an encouragement and hope in a world that is hopeless and full of discouragement!

Prayer

Heavenly Father,

Please forgive me for the times I have not held on to Your word and the teachings of Jesus, Your prophets and apostles. Give me a teachable heart so that I may grow in the knowledge of Your Holy word. Establish Your word within my heart so that I may teach others Your truth. You are my only Hope – a hope that is desperately needed in this world with so much pain and hopelessness. Help me to remember that truth every day and to remain focused on You.

In Your name, Jesus,

Amen

Day Nine

1 Thessalonians 5:19-21

"Do not quench the Spirit. Do not despise prophecies. Test all things; hold fast what is good. Abstain from every form of evil."

Do you know how to quench the Spirit? I have read that when we don't love, when we hold on to grudges and we choose to not forgive others, we quench the Holy Spirit in our lives. We also quench the Holy Spirit when we doubt and don't believe God's truth. We quench it when we begin to ignore His Spirit like we no longer need it. We quench the Holy Spirit in others when we discourage them. I wonder if we begin quenching when we no longer hold fast to what is good – what is godly. I really noticed this when an ungodly relationship was eliminated in my life. I had learned that the person in this unhealthy friendship had embraced a sinful lifestyle, one that could be easily hidden, but was evil and ungodly nonetheless. Shortly afterwards, the friendship ended. I do wonder if this person felt my disapproval what she and her husband had gotten themselves into. While the termination of that friendship broke my heart, I quickly realized just how much the Holy Spirit had been quenched in my life. As my heart healed, God began to move in my life in ways I never fathomed. My faith deepened, my emotional and mental strength escalated, God's voice was clearer than it ever had been. He led me into ministries I by no means contemplated before. Finally, the Holy Spirit was free to do as the Father willed. It is incredibly amazing!! So, are you prepared to find out how you are quenching the Spirit? Are you holding onto something that isn't godly? Are you ready to let go of it and allow the Holy Spirit to do amazing things through you? I can tell you – it is so worth the loss of ungodly things to have the godly.

Prayer

Heavenly Father,

Please forgive me for the times I have quenched Your spirit – either by being unloving, by harbouring bitterness, by ignoring You or by holding on to the ungodly. Please show me now the things in my life that are quenching Your Spirit so that I may let them go and hold fast to what is good. Give me the courage to let those things go, to hand them over to You. I so desire to be Your instrument, tune me to Your song. Please, Holy Spirit, come and work through my life. Do as you please, Father.

In Jesus' name,

Amen

Day Ten

Hebrews 3:5-6

"And Moses indeed was faithful in all His house as a servant, for a testimony of those things which would be spoken afterward, but Christ as a Son over His own house, whose house we are if we hold fast the confidence and the rejoicing of the hope firm to the end."

Moses was a servant in the house, the temple. But Jesus built the house. So, here, we are learning that Jesus is superior to Moses – and Moses was a pretty good guy. But Jesus is exalted far above Moses. We know that the Jewish people held Moses in very high esteem, as they should. Moses was saved as a baby, raised as a prince of Egypt. He then found out who he really was and he returned to his people, rescuing them out of slavery.

Jesus, the Son of God, should then be held higher than Moses. He is the One who rescues and saves from slavery. But, have you ever doubted who you were? The Hebrews were doubting, so the writer of Hebrews is reassuring them that they are indeed, part of the family of God and they just need to keep hanging on – holding fast to their confidence in Christ – in His plan of salvation. Hold fast to His plan, to the hope we have in Him.

This is such a good reminder to us. We can get so caught up in our feelings and our circumstances. We can get caught up in how others treat us or how they have wronged us. But just keep looking up – into the face of Jesus. Hold on tight to His hand. He will never let go – you are a child of God.

Prayer

Heavenly Father,

Thank You so much for the promise of being in Your family, being Your child. Please forgive me for the times I have been discouraged and relied upon my own feelings. Please help me to fully trust in You and to hold tight to Your hand. Never let me forget that I am a part of Your family as are my brothers and sisters in Christ.

In Your Name, Jesus,

Amen

Day Eleven

Hebrews 10:23

"Let us hold fast the confession of *our* hope without wavering, for He who promised *is* faithful."

Isn't it so incredibly amazing that we are able to approach the throne of the Almighty God whenever and wherever we wish? No matter what, we can go to Him. But there are times when we waver, isn't there? Like when we have sinned. I know for me, when I have sinned – especially if it is the same sin I seem to repeat over and over – I feel so ashamed I don't want to go to the throne. I am so unworthy. I don't believe that He is willing to forgive me again...and again. So I pull away. I sit in my own filth, helpless. Finally, after a while (sometimes it is a long while), I realize it isn't about me or what I have done. It isn't about the sin I am struggling with. It isn't the fact that I struggle with sin. In fact, it is never even about how 'good' I am on my respectable, virtuous days. Even on my absolute best day, full of obedience and love, I am still unworthy to come to the Holy of Holies on my own. It is ONLY because of what Christ has done that I can even contemplate approaching my Heavenly Father. The idea that He sent His one and only Son to earth to die for my sins just so that I could freely – and without shame – come to Him. He knew I'd mess up daily – even many times a day – and that I would have to sit at His feet often. And He desires the same thing – He longs for me to come to Him every day. He yearns for you to come to Him, too. It's not based on what you've done or haven't done – either in obedience or disobedience – it is because of Christ.

I am getting better at not hiding from Him, working at not running away, ashamed. I will come to my Father with my head hung low. And He gently puts His hand beneath my chin and lifts my face to look at Him. And I see the gentlest, loving eyes; a welcoming smile. I see His relief that I didn't hold off any longer. And He tells me I am His and there is absolutely nothing I could do or not do that would prohibit me from coming to Him.

So, come. Hold fast to Him who is faithful. Run to His throne room. Don't stop.

Prayer

Heavenly Father,

It is utterly amazing that You loved me so much that You provided a way for me to enter into Your Holy presence. Please forgive me for the times I have hidden in my shame instead of running to You. Help me to remember that it is only because of what Your Son has done on the cross that I am able to boldly come to You. Thank You so much that You have made a way for me to come to You, that You pursue me and long for me. I long to be in Your presence.

In the name of Jesus,

Amen

Day Twelve

1 Peter 5:9

"Resist him, steadfast in the faith, knowing that the same sufferings are experienced by your brotherhood in the world."

Here, we are being warned about out adversary, Satan. He walks around purposefully looking for someone to devour. What comes to mind with the word devour? I think of a wild animal that is so hungry, it viciously tears into flesh and doesn't stop eating until there is nothing left. I don't think this idea is too farfetched when it comes to our enemy. He is ruthless. He doesn't care how old we are or what we are going through. He doesn't care if we are a child, an adult or a senior. He doesn't care if we are already wounded. He hates us. Do you get that? He absolutely HATES us. He hates every human being - even the ones who worship him. He is the opposite of Christ. Christ is love, He is the definition of love. Satan is fully hatred, the epitome of despise. For the follower of Christ, the enemy lurks about, he waits patiently and quietly, always ready for attack. He watches for a chink in our armour, he is always watching for his moment to destroy. This isn't always evident for us, most likely it is rarely obvious when he deceives us. That's why Paul tells us to be sober and vigilant. That's why he tells us to remain steadfast in our faith. So that we may resist the devil and make him flee from us. It is vital for us to be steadfast in the word of God in our battles, the word of God is our sword and it is what will defeat our enemy. Jesus used scripture to fight off Satan. We need to use scripture as well. We also need to be aware that Satan knows the word of God and will use his twisted version of it to try and throw us off course. It is imperative for us to KNOW God's word so well that we are confident in our knowledge of Satan's lies about God's word.

It is also encouraging to know that we aren't alone in this battle. Our fellow brothers and sisters are in full armour as well and are fighting alongside us. We can be on the other side of the world and engage in battle for our brothers and sisters on another continent! We do this through prayer! What do we do when a brother or sister has been wounded in the fight? Do we leave them there to die? Absolutely not! Never, ever leave a soldier in the battlefield! Our shields of faith are defensive weapons, they are HUGE and they are meant to work with other shields of faith to protect ourselves and our comrades. Place your shield of faith over your comrade until they have rested and recovered from the wounding enough to wield their sword again and hold their shield up.

Prayer

Heavenly Father,

Thank You for Your word and the warning and admonitions within it. Through Your word, You have given me more than enough to live a victorious life over my enemy. Help me to stand fast in my faith and to be fully equipped for war. Help me to be sober and vigilant so that I won't be devoured by my enemy. Put people into my life who will fight alongside me and put their shield of faith over me when necessary. Knit us together so that we may fight for each other. Thank You for sword of Your spirit and that You have fully equipped us for battle. Thank You that the armour I wear is the very same armour Jesus wears himself.

In Your precious name, Jesus,

Amen

Day Thirteen

Hebrews 10:23

"Let us hold fast the confession of our hope without wavering, for He who promised is faithful."

Verse 10 says we have been sanctified through Jesus Christ once and for all. There are no exceptions, no exclusions. No hypothetical situations. It says once and for all! That is our HOPE! Let's not waver in that. If He said it, He meant it. The offering for our sin has been accomplished. Why do we hang on to sin the way we do? Why do we live in shame and guilt over things we have confessed and repented of? We have the remarkable opportunity to approach the awesome throne of God – think about that for a minute. Because Jesus' death tore the veil that separated the Holy of Holies from the rest of the temple, we are able to boldly go to God. Previous to His death, no one could, except the High Priest once a year. But now, any one of us may enter the Holy of Holies and kneel at the throne of God. The veil is now His flesh (v. 20). So, be daring and confident, enter the Holy of Holies, confess and repent – and receive forgiveness. This is our hope – hold fast to it! Our enemy longs to steal this confidence from us. He lies to us telling us our sin is too great. But no, it isn't. No sin is too great – it has already been placed upon His shoulders when He was hanging on the cross. Hold fast to this truth because if you don't, that snake will steal and destroy. God is faithful to the end of time.

Prayer

Heavenly Father, thank You so much that You have allowed us to enter into your presence with confidence. Thank You that You are faithful to forgive us our sins when we ask. Right now, I confess any sin in my life that is separating me from You. Reveal to me any sin that I may have overlooked. Help me to run to Your throne when life is overwhelming. Help me to hold fast to Your promise of faithfulness and forgiveness, that I will not waver in the promise of Your redemption.

In the name of Jesus,

Amen

Day Fourteen

Hebrews 3:14

"For we have become partakers of Christ if we hold the beginning of our confidence steadfast to the end."

We are partakers OF Christ – as well as with Christ as is stated clearly in other passages of scripture – but this verse says OF Christ. Who is He? He is love, mercy, redemption, grace, wise, righteousness, restoration and sanctification. He is the fullness of God. And we are partakers of that! To be able to stand before God, covered by His precious blood, and Jesus, having accomplished this, sits at the right hand of God. We stand before them both. There is so much to contemplate when we consider that we are partakers of Christ – so much that it becomes incomprehensible. To be a partaker, we must live off of Christ, we must be nourished by Him – constantly. He is our hope. We must remain steadfast in this truth – to be partakers of Christ is the beginning of our confidence.

Prayer

Heavenly Father, thank you so much for giving me the privilege of partaking of Your Son, Jesus. Please help me to stand fast in this truth and have confidence in Your word.

In Your name, Jesus,

Amen

Day Fifteen

Deuteronomy 11:22, 23

"'For if you carefully keep all these commandments which I command you to do—to love the LORD your God, to walk in all His ways, and to hold fast to Him—'then the LORD will drive out all these nations from before you, and you will dispossess greater and mightier nations than yourselves."

We are under a new covenant under Christ, the old covenant has been eliminated through His death and resurrection. But I think the fact that we need to hold fast to God is still relevant. We still need to walk in His ways and we need to fulfill the greatest commandment – to LOVE Him with all our heart, mind, soul and strength. Do you love Him like that? I wonder...if we love Him like that, does that mean we are holding fast to Him? If we are walking in His ways, are we holding fast? When we hold fast to Him, we live in VICTORY! This is the victorious life of the disciple of Christ!

This doesn't mean we won't face trials or difficult times. It just means that through those hard times, as we cling to Jesus, we can be confident that we will make it through. We won't just survive or barely make it through. We will be victorious! We will overcome because we have the Overcomer on our side. He has already won the victory! We will end up having a deeper relationship, love and devotion to Jesus as He leads us through the tough times.

Prayer

Heavenly Father, thank you so much for the promise of victory we have when we hold fast to You. Please help me to love You as Your Son commanded, to walk in Your ways and to hold on to You desperately.

In Your precious name,

Amen

Day Sixteen

Deuteronomy 4:4

"But you who held fast to the LORD your God are alive today, every one of you."

In this passage, God had destroyed the Israelites who were worshipping Baal instead of Him. The Israelites who continued to worship the one true God were spared. When we worship false idols, we find emptiness and 'death' in our spirits. Some of those false idols may satisfy us temporarily, but that satisfaction soon fades away and we need to find a new idol to worship. The God of the Bible is the only One who is able to fulfill our needs and desires forever. He is the One who gives us LIFE abundantly through His Son, Jesus. We have life because we hold fast to Him.

What false idols have you been chasing? Who or what have you been looking to for fulfillment? Your spouse? I have done that. I have looked to my husband to 'complete me'. The truth is; he cannot. He is human and he will make mistakes. The only One who is able to complete me is the One who made me. I must not worship my husband this way. What about friends? We can also look to friendships for identity. They cannot tell me who I am and they do not deserve my worship. Are you chasing money and wealth? Have you fallen for the prosperity gospel? I did. It is so enticing, yet so elusive. And a big LIE!

Be sure that you are worshipping God and God alone. This is not a onetime check – but something that needs to be scrutinized regularly. He is the only One who deserves out worship.

Prayer

Heavenly Father, please forgive me for the times I have searched elsewhere for fulfillment in my soul. You are the only One who can satisfy the deep longings within my soul. Please help me to hold fast to You for life.

In Your precious name,

Amen

Day Seventeen

Deuteronomy 10:20, 21

"You shall fear the LORD your God; you shall serve Him, and to Him you shall hold fast, and take oaths in His name. He *is* your praise, and He *is* your God, who has done for you these great and awesome things which your eyes have seen."

Oh, to fear the Lord. In the last several years or so, the idea of fearing God has been tamed somewhat. I've heard it explained as a high respect for God. But when I contemplate this idea a bit more, I realize that, just as God's word says, no one has been able to see the face of God. Moses was the closest one – but he had to hide his face as God passed by him – that was all he could handle. Then I think about the tabernacle and the Holy of Holies. Only the High Priest could enter into the Holy of Holies – and only once a year – and only if his sins were repented of – otherwise he'd be struck dead. That would cause me fear and trembling! Then there was the guy who touched the Ark of the Covenant because it was falling over. What happened to him? Just because he touched the Ark – the box that held the covenant between God and man (even just that idea evokes more than a deep respect!), he was killed. If that wouldn't impart true FEAR into the hearts of those around, I don't know what would! So, yes, I do believe the fear mentioned in scripture is a real, true, colossal fear of God. Not a sweetened version of it. Now, for those who do not live under this new covenant, that's an entirely different story. They should fear – for their souls.

BUT...we have a NEW covenant. We need not be afraid to approach the Holy of Holies! This is exciting! We don't have to be a high priest – we are best friends with the

Ultimate High Priest! We may approach more than once a year, in fact He prefers that we approach daily – many times a day! We won't die when we approach, in fact, when we do approach and we take our sins and hurts to our loving Father, we come ALIVE! Let's hold fast to this promise! Let Him be our praise and worship! Let Him be our God! Our eyes have seen all of the wonderful things He has done for us, let's hold fast to them and not forget it.

Prayer

Heavenly Father,

Thank you so much that you have made a new covenant with me so that I may come into the Holy of Holies without fear. Thank you for sacrificing Your Son so that I may come before you with my pain, sin and praise. I pray for my loved ones who do not know Christ. I pray that I will be a brightly shining beacon of your love and mercy. Please help me to remember all You have done for me.

In Your name,

Amen

Day Eighteen

Deuteronomy 13:4

"You shall walk after the LORD your God and fear Him, and keep His commandments and obey His voice; you shall serve Him and hold fast to Him. "

What does it mean to walk after the Lord? I am reminded of that scene in "The Lion King" when Simba is following his father. Simba and his friend Nala ventured into dangerous territory, their lives were threatened. Mufasa came to their rescue and the cubs followed him back home. Simba is walking behind his dad and he suddenly steps in his father's foot imprint. Simba realizes how much bigger his dad's print is than his tiny paw. Mufasa's paws are gigantic and protective. Simba understands at this point that his dad knows what is best for him and he should continue to follow him.

God's 'footprints' are massive; so much bigger than we can fathom. Let's hold on to His protective hands. He knows what is best for us. He wants to lead us away from soul threatening places. He is making the way for us. Serve Him, obey Him, keep His word.

Prayer

Heavenly Father,

Thank you for making a way for me. In every situation, You are always leading me and guiding me, walking before me. Please forgive me for those times I have strayed from Your 'footprints' because I did not trust You. Help me to trust You completely and fully.

In Your precious name,

Amen

Day Nineteen

Deuteronomy 30:20

"That you may love the LORD your God, that you may obey His voice, and that you may cling to Him, for He *is* your life and the length of your days; and that you may dwell in the land which the LORD swore to your fathers, to Abraham, Isaac, and Jacob, to give them."

What a fantastic verse!! I love how it says to CLING to Him! He is our life, so cling to Him! In the verse before, we are instructed to choose life; and that life is in God. We must choose Him! We choose to love Him, to obey

Him and to seize His hand. This is our choice. He isn't going to intrude on our will. He delights in giving us blessing after blessing. He desires for us to dwell in Him, in His blessing. We dwell in Him when we hang on to Him for life. God already knows what we will choose, but it is our responsibility to choose Him; and to keep choosing Him. The other option is death and curses. That's the opposite of life and blessing. That is not what I want for my time here on earth. It is not the heritage I want to leave my children and my grandchildren...and so on. I choose LIFE. Do you?

Prayer

Heavenly Father,

Thank you so much for offering me life and blessing. I understand that this is my choice and I willingly choose to follow and obey You. Please forgive me for not always taking my responsibility in this decision seriously. Please help me to dwell in Your presence and to always choose life and blessing.

In Your name,

Amen

Day Twenty

Joshua 22:5

"But take careful heed to do the commandment and the law which Moses the servant of the LORD commanded you, to love the LORD your God, to walk in all His ways, to keep His commandments, to hold fast to Him, and to serve Him with all your heart and with all your soul."

God knew we could not keep His commands. He knew that we would fail every time. He had a plan right from the beginning that would save us because He knew we wouldn't be able to keep His commands. The 10 Commandments remind us of this fact – we are incapable of keeping them day in and day out. Jesus is the bridge, He fills the gap between us and God. He narrows down the 10 Commandments into 2 commandments. The first being that we should love God with all of our hearts, minds, souls and strength. The second is to love others as ourselves. We still need the Saviour, though, don't we? But, as we continue to hold fast to Him, the more like Him we become. The more like Him we are, the more we will love God and love others. And the more we love and adore Him, the less we fall into sin. Find reference

Let's serve Him with all of our hearts and souls! Let's do the work of the Lord. That's the only work that truly matters anyway.

Prayer

Heavenly Father,

Thank you so much that You provided a way for me to follow You and to love You, through your Son. Please forgive me for the times I have tried to please You on my own with my own works. Please help me to be more like Jesus, loving you and loving others.

In Your precious name,

Amen

Day Twenty-One

Joshua 23:8

"But you shall hold fast to The Lord your God, as you have done to this day."

I like to keep a journal. I don't write in it daily, but when I feel like I need to write something down. My entries are mostly during times of struggle. Quite a few months ago, I was reading through one of my first journals to get notes for a talk I was preparing for. Sometimes, I have these brilliant epiphanies! As I looked through my writings, I could see the hand of God in my life. I saw how He had brought me out of turmoil and distress. I saw how He answered my cries for rescue and healing. It was amazing! I was holding fast to God during those times, He was all I had to hang on to, after all. This passage in Joshua is a reminder of the things God had done for His people. Joshua was old at this time. It seems he was preparing the Israelites for his departure from earth. He keeps reminding them of their history, what God brought them through. Encouraging them to hold on to God's law and promises, to follow Him. He reminds them that it was God who fought for them in battle, that God defeated their enemies. He reminds them to be courageous...something Joshua frequently tells the Israelites throughout. It is so important for us to remember what God has brought us through and to hang on to His promise that He will continue to do so.

Prayer

Heavenly Father,

Thank you for all that you have brought me through (name some specific situations here). I know Your promises never fail and that You will always bring me through any situation before me. I am struggling with this situation now (be specific, name what you are going through). You promise to make a way for me. I will wait for Your promise. I thank you for all of the blessings in my life right now. I especially thank you for (name the blessings in your life; continue to think on them throughout your day). Please help me to have courage and to hold on to Your amazing promises.

In the name of Jesus,

Amen

Day Twenty-Two

Acts 11:23 KJV

"Who, when he came, and had seen the grace of God, was glad, and exhorted them all, that with purpose of heart they would cleave unto the Lord."

This was after the persecution that occurred after Stephen's death. Believers were afraid and many taught to only the Jews. But some were preaching to the Hellenists in Antioch, of whom many turned to Christ. The believers in Jerusalem sent Barnabas to Antioch to find out what was happening and Barnabas saw that God was working there and encouraged the people to cling to God. I love the idea of clinging to God. I picture desperation and urgency. Clinging to The Lord in desperation and urgency during the tough times of life. This is what we are supposed to be doing at all times. Not just during difficult times, but during times when life seems to be perfect and everything just falls into place. How are you clinging to your Saviour today? Are you barely hanging on? Or is your grasp firm and confident? I have experienced both ways myself. I have found that the times when I am barely hanging on are the times when Jesus is really making sure I don't lose my grip. And the times when my hold is confident are the times when Jesus is still holding tight. Be encouraged in this truth, that Jesus never lets go, even when we feel like we already have. He is always there.

Prayer

Heavenly Father,

Thank you so much for holding on to me and never letting go. Please help me to trust Your promise that You are always there for me even when I don't feel Your presence. Please help me to see Your hand in my life. Also help others to see the work You are doing in my life so as to bring You glory and to bring others to You.

In Your name Jesus,

Amen

Day Twenty-Three

Romans 12:9-13

"Let love be without hypocrisy. Abhor what is evil. Cling to what is good. Be kindly affectionate to one another with brotherly love, in honor giving preference to one another; not lagging in diligence, fervent in spirit, serving The Lord; rejoicing in hope, patient in tribulation, continuing steadfastly in prayer; distributing to the needs of the saints, given to hospitality."

We have 2 points of holding fast in this passage. The first is the admonition to cling to what is good. What is good? First, let's take a look at the two statements beforehand. We must not be hypocritical in our love. Have you ever seen someone being hypocritical with their love? Have you ever been? How is one hypocritical with love?

Abhor what is evil. I'm not sure if there is a heavier word for hate than abhor. When I reflect in that word, I feel like it is worse than hate, it is deeper than just hate. This is how we are to view anything from the evil one; any kind of sin that he has developed in order to divide us from God. I read something recently that felt like premarital sex was a trivial matter, that it didn't matter too much if you made a mistake and had sex before marriage because Jesus will forgive and restore anyway. Yes, He will forgive and He will restore...but I felt like the author was implying that the death and resurrection of my sweet Saviour gave people a license to sin. The fact that real consequences to mistakes are inescapable, especially consequences of sexual sin, is accurate. Sadly, I know this firsthand. Paul tells us to HATE anything evil. Premarital sex is our enemy's lie and tactic to keep us separated from God. Don't go through life believing that you can choose to sin because it will be forgiven anyway. There will still be consequences.

Paul wants us to cling to what is good. Jesus is good. Every perfect gift comes from the Father of Lights. Let us hang on to what is good and true. And part of that is being affectionate to those in the family of God. This is good.

Paul tells us to continue steadfastly in prayer. Sometimes we get tired of praying for certain things or certain people when we don't see any progress being made. But we don't see what is going on behind the scenes, do we? What seems like eternity for us is only fleeting moments for God. We need to continuously remind ourselves that God is ultimately in control of everything. His Spirit prepares hearts, not us. He changes people and situations, not us. We do our part, yes, but in the end, only He is the One who answers prayer. Prayer is so much more effective than anything else. I firmly believe this. There are situations that we cannot do anything about, isn't there? But when we pray and the Spirit of God begins to move, things begin to change. It might take time to notice this change, but it is happening. Even if it is just in our own hearts. Don't lose heart in your prayer times. God is working, He is doing something. Rest in that truth.

Prayer

Heavenly Father,

Thank you that there is good in this world. That despite the ruling of the evil one, You are still in full control and Your goodness is evident. Please forgive me for the times I have become disparaged from all of the evil. Forgive me for the times I have minimized evil and have given license to sin. Forgive me for the times I have become discouraged in my prayer life instead of trusting Your word. Please help me to live a life of goodness and truth. Bless me in my prayer time with You, draw me so close to You during those times.

In Your precious name Jesus,

Amen

Day Twenty-Four

1 Corinthians 15:58

"Therefore, my beloved brethren, be steadfast, immovable, always abounding in the work of The Lord, knowing that your labor is not in vain in The Lord."

Here, Paul is encouraging us to be steadfast in God's work, doing the things we are called to do. God's work is never in vain. It can feel like that though sometimes, can't it? We feel like we aren't doing any good in our area of ministry. We are tired, maybe even a little disgruntled - we get caught up with these types of questions...why don't so-and-so do anything? Why do all of these people come to church Sunday mornings and do nothing else during the week? This is the wrong thinking! When we begin thinking this way, we tend to miss what God is doing through US. I need regular reminders of this. Especially when my husband is gone often for church related work (I also have to remember how blessed I am that he works from home and I see him all day long).

We have to continue steadfastly doing what God has called Us to do and not worry about someone else's life, or lack of ministry work. We don't know what is going on in their lives, where God needs to do work. Actually, we can feel blessed and thankful that God has bestowed such awesome responsibility upon us. We can be honoured that He would trust us with such a ministry. Even if we need to be reminded of it daily.

Prayer

Heavenly Father,

Thank you so much for the ministry work you have given to me to do. It is such an honour to work for You and to further Your kingdom. Please forgive me for the times I have made ministry work about me or about what others are not doing. Please forgive me of my pride in this area. Please help me to remain steadfast in the work You have given me. Please help me to continue furthering Your kingdom and sharing the truth of the gospel to those who need to hear it. Please bless the work of my hands and be glorified through it.

In Your precious name Jesus,

Amen

Day Twenty-Five

Psalm 136:1 ESV

"Give thanks to the LORD, for He is good,
for His steadfast love endures forever."

This whole chapter of Psalms talks about the steadfast love of God. I know I need this kind of repeated reminder of His love for me – His steadfast love that endures FOREVER! I often doubt His love for me. When I don't 'feel' it or when life seems to go haywire. I tend to not believe His word and His promises. Doubt creeps in and can become rooted within my heart. This weed affects every part of my life. I soon begin to doubt my husband's love for me. I doubt the love between me and my children. I doubt the love my friends have for me.

When I am confident in His love for me, I can weather the storms of life easier. I also am more confident in Marcus' love for me. Have you ever noticed this? I find it fascinating! When I know and trust in God's love for me, I am so much more confident in my love for Marcus and his love for me. It is like a ripple effect – we begin with the most important love of our lives – or who is supposed to be the most important – and the love and confidence extends from Him!

The next time you are feeling unloved by someone close to you – especially your husband or a dear friend – check in on how you are trusting in His love for you.

Prayer

Heavenly Father,

Please forgive me for the times I have not trusted in Your steadfast love for me; a love that endures forever. Please help me to grow confident in Your love for me, knowing without hesitation or doubt that Your love for me is endless and knows no end. Please help me to grow in Your love so that my love for others and my confidence in their love for me grows deeper. Thank You so much for Your love.

In the name of Jesus,

Amen

Day Twenty-Six

Titus 1:9

"Holding fast to the faithful word as he has been taught, that he may be able, by sound doctrine, both to exhort and convict those who contradict."

Paul is setting up the leaders in the church. In this section, he is talking about bishops. He lists the qualities of a bishop, which really are things we should strive for in our lives as well. A bishop should be blameless, or carry the righteousness of Christ. He should be doing the will of God, not his own will. He should not have a temper or be a drunk. He should not be violent or greedy for money. He should be hospitable, love good things, reasonable, just, holy and self-controlled. Those are high standards, especially these days! A bishop should also hold fast to what he has been taught so that he can exhort and convict in a biblical manner. A bishop is a person in leadership, someone who teaches and leads others. He needs to be able to know the word of God and apply it to his life, to live a life that honours God. We all have someone who looks up to us, someone who watches how we behave. This person is either a Christian or someone who doesn't know Christ. They watch how we live. And they either follow our footsteps, our leading; or they watch to see if they can find fault. I know, for some who really want to find fault, they will find it whether it is there or not. But the point is to know and understand that somehow, we are mentoring someone, regardless of whether or not we want to. We may not officially be a bishop within our church, but we are representatives of Christ to all. Let's hold on tightly to the word of God so that we may consistently lead others to Christ.

Prayer

Heavenly Father,

Please forgive me for the times I haven't lived in a way that honours You. Please help me to be all of those good things that Paul has listed here. Help me to reflect Your glory in my life. I know that there will be people who will always find fault no matter what I do and I ask that You will help me to forgive them and just continue giving You the glory. I just want to point others to You, Jesus.

Please help me to hold on so tightly to You that there will never be any doubt from whom my strength comes from.

In Your sweet name, Jesus,

Amen

Day Twenty-Seven

Colossians 2:2-5

"...that their hearts may be encouraged, being knit together in love, and attaining to all riches of the full assurance of understanding, to the knowledge of the mystery of God, both of the Father and of Christ, in whom are hidden all the treasures of wisdom and knowledge.

Now this I say lest anyone should deceive you with persuasive words. For though I am absent in the flesh, yet I am with you in spirit, rejoicing to see your good order and the steadfastness of your faith in Christ."

We are so bombarded with the health, wealth and beauty 'gospel' these days, aren't we? And it can be so easy to be trapped in that web. But in this passage, Paul reassures the Colossians to be pursuing the riches of the knowledge of the mysteries of God. He tells us to be encouraged within our hearts. We must have heavenly prosperity, which far surpasses any amount of earthly prosperity. Our souls prosper when we grow in the knowledge of God's mysteries, when we grow in our relationship with Christ.

Because it is so easy to be entrapped in worldly thinking and philosophies, we must be very wary of those who teach opposite of heavenly prosperity. Paul says we should not be deceived by their persuasive words – and some sure can be persuasive!! They will use guilt and shame to brainwash us into their ideology and false teachings. The only way to prevent this is to be steadfast in our faith. We must be growing continuously in our faith and relationship with Christ.

Let's keep reminding each other of this truth! Let's continue to speak truth to each other.

Prayer

Heavenly Father,

Thank You so much that I don't have to strive for earthly riches here on earth. That lifestyle eventually becomes so cumbersome and empty. Please forgive me for those times I have become envious of what others have and not content with what You have given to me.

Please forgive me for the times I have fallen for the false gospel of earthly prosperity. Please help me to live for You and for soul prosperity. Please let Your light shine so brightly through me that people will be directed to You instead of worldly people.

In Your precious name Jesus,

Amen

Day Twenty-Eight

2 Peter 3:17, 18

"You therefore, beloved, since you know this beforehand, beware lest you also fall from your own steadfastness, being lead away with the error of the wicked; but grow in the grace and knowledge of our Lord and Savior Jesus Christ."

Peter is warning us to be very careful to whom we listen to. He tells us to keep our focus on Jesus and to remember Paul's wisdom in the scriptures because there are parts of scripture that are hard to understand and people who do not have a strong understanding of God's word will twist these passages as they have done with other parts of scripture. We don't have to be followers of Christ for very long to see how God's word can get twisted. And if we are really honest, we will admit to doing these ourselves from time to time. We will put our own twist on God's word in order to justify our beliefs, our thinking, and our choices. I know I have tried to do this myself at one point or another. But I always knew it was wrong - I felt the Holy Spirit's conviction. It is scary enough to think that I can so easily manipulate the word of God, but even scarier to think that some people are so far gone from the presence of God that they no longer feel the conviction. I never want to be separated from God so much that I no longer sense that conviction. I don't want to twist His word for my own agenda. Here, Peter is warning us, we have no excuse in this matter. He says because we know this will happen we need to grow in the grace of Jesus so that we do not fall for our own steadfastness. That is something to consider, we can't be so steadfast that we cannot fall from it. We can still be lead away by false teachers at any point. We cannot simply rely on our own steadfastness to keep us safe from those who unabashedly twist the word of God. We must grow in the grace AND wisdom of Christ Jesus. This is a process, one that doesn't t end. We must keep going.

Prayer

Heavenly Father,

Please forgive me for the times I have listened to those who have not spoken complete truth, even myself. Please forgive me for the times I have twisted Your Holy Word in order to justify my own actions. Please help me to never be so lost that I do not sense the conviction of Your Holy Spirit. Help me to not rely on my own steadfastness, which is a facade anyway. I have no steadfastness apart from You. Thank You so much that I need only trust in you and Your faithfulness in order to be steadfast in my faith.

In Your name Jesus,

Amen

Day Twenty-Nine

1 Corinthians 16:13, 14

"Watch, stand fast in the faith, be brave, be strong. Let all that you do be done with love."

This is such a great encouragement to us. Paul reminds us be watchful and to stand fast in our faith. Have you ever felt like you were losing your faith? I've been there. I thought that I was losing my faith. I saw it crumbling before my eyes. Or so I thought. I struggled with these questions "is there really a God? Have I believed in something for so long that isn't even true?". I struggled with this for quite some time. I finally realized that I couldn't give up on something I had believed in for so long. Then I struggled with whether or not Jesus cared about me enough do help me through what I was going through. I really thought I was losing the faith I had held onto for so long. One day as I was driving home, I felt God speaking to my heart about my struggle. He said 'Aimee, you are not losing your faith. I am tearing it down so I can build you a new one. One that is so strong it will be like a burning ember within you." As I look back on that time in my life, I can honestly say that God is so faithful. The faith I have now is so much stronger and deeper than ever before. So, if you are struggling, stand fast in the faith that you have – even if it is just so small. God is building it up. Be brave, be strong. God will lead you through this time and you will be amazed at what He has done in your life. It takes time and patience, but it is so worth it. Hang in there. It is only for a season.

One thing that helped my faith to grow was having faith for others. I found that to be so much easier than having faith for myself. I continued to pray with and for people. I could muster more faith for them than for myself. And, really, that was a very good thing! It was a start, it was a place to begin to rebuild. Over time, I saw the evidence of my growing faith. Continue to pray for others and speak into their lives.

Prayer

Heavenly Father,

Some days I don't know how much longer I can hang on. Sometimes I feel like my faith is gone, obliterated. Please help me to trust that You are building my faith even when I don't see it or feel it. Please help me to hang on to Your promises. Turn my faith into a glowing ember deep within my soul. Bring people into my life who will encourage me and help to build my faith. Bring people into my life whom I can pray for, people who won't overwhelm me with their problems, but those I can have faith for and You can begin rebuilding my faith.

In the name of Jesus,

Amen

Day Thirty

Hebrews 2:2, 3

"For if the word spoken through angels proved steadfast and every transgression and disobedience received a just reward, how shall we escape if we neglect so great a salvation which at the first began to be spoken by The Lord, and was confirmed to us by those who heard Him."

In verse 1, we are being warned to not fall for false teachings; we must not compromise the truth. There is so much pressure from the world to compromise the gospel isn't there? We are told that we are 'haters' because we stick to the word of God. Or we are accused of being judgmental (so, judging has become much worse than the sin being committed and called out).

The word spoken through angels is the law that Moses gave. If we don't place our trust in Jesus, we cannot escape punishment for our sin. The law will remain steadfast if our trust and faith are not in Christ. How many times have you heard "if I am good enough, I'll get to heaven." Or "She was a good person. She is surely in heaven". These individuals are choosing to live by the law instead of the grace of God. The law spoken through angels will offer a swift and just 'reward' for those in disobedience and transgression of the law. I know there is no way I would be able to be good enough to follow the law of Moses. No way! I have lied. I have cheated. I have stolen. I have hated. I have murdered within my heart. I have been envious. I have taken God's name in vain. I've had false idols. I have worshipped other things and people instead of God. Do I need to go on? I need the gospel message in my life! I need redemption from Jesus Christ! He is the ONLY way to the Father! There is no way I am getting into heaven on my own! And, really, isn't that a relief? I no longer have to strive or become overwhelmed with trying so hard. I just need to rest in the truth of my salvation through Jesus Christ. He has done it all for me. He has paid the price for me. May I never neglect the salvation spoken by my Father – there will be no escape if I do. His word proves to be steadfast – all of it.

Prayer

Heavenly Father,

Thank You so much that You have provided a way for me to come to You so I don't have to strive endlessly for Your love and acceptance. It is freely given through Your Son, Jesus. Please forgive me for the times I have disobeyed Your Word and Your law. Forgive me for the times I have not loved with all of my heart, mind, soul and strength and I have not loved my neighbour as myself. Please help me to grow in these areas and to live fully for You. Your sacrifice was so great, may I never minimize what You have given to me.

In Your name Jesus,

Amen

Thank you for purchasing Hold Fast: A 30-Day Devotional. I hope you enjoyed it and I pray you were greatly blessed through it.

Please visit my website: aimeeimbeau.com

Or visit me on facebook:
facebook.com/Aimee.Imbeau.Ministry

I can be found on Twitter and Pinterest under my name.

I would love to hear from you!

Blessings,

Aimee

Made in the USA
Charleston, SC
10 January 2015